Holy Ghost FIRE Talk (Volume 1)

EVANGELIST KING

ISBN-13: 978-0692463048 (The Children's Mite)
ISBN-10: 0692463046

DEDICATION

To those who inspired me to compose my messages into a book. Thanks for the encouragement. Shalom †

CONTENTS

Acknowledgements   i

Can a TRUE Christian Have a Demon?   1
    The Popular Belief   1
    Am I a True Christian?   1
    What is Sin?   3
    Delegated Authority   3
    Rebellion is Witchcraft   4
    Submissive to God   5
    My Damascus Experience   6
    Your Helper   10

PESTERING Faith   11
    What is Pestering Faith?   11
    How to Pray?   12
    PESTERING Faith Keep Asking   13
    PESTERING Faith Keep Seeking   14
    PESTERING Faith Keep Knocking   14
    The Canaanite Woman   15
    Prayer   20

Maintaining Your Deliverance   21
    SUBMIT (to God)   21
    RESIST (the Devil)   22
    FLEE (the Devil)   23
    Yesterday, Today and Forever   23
    Testimony   24
    In Conclusion   24
    Prayer   26

Set Your Affection   27
    Focus On Things Above   27
    Where is Our Affection?   28
    Words Reflect the Heart   29
    It Begins at Home   30
    No Earthly Good? To Who?   31
    Testimony   32

FIRE Prayers against Spirit Spouses (and friends)   33
    What are Spirit Spouses?   33
    What are FIRE Prayers?   33
    Survey Questions   34
    FIRE Prayers   35
    Contact Us   37
    Words of Encouragement   37
    Prayer   38
    Testimonies   38

FIRE Prayer for Pregnancy   41
    Don't Delay Obedience   41
    All Have Sinned   42
    FIRE Prayers   43
    Testimony   45
    In Conclusion   46

Deliverance Prayer   48

ACKNOWLEDGEMENTS

Thank you to the following individuals who without their contributions and support this book would not have been written:

Roger, Helen, Debi, Murial, Janelle

AND

TCM's Donors

Shalom †

CAN A TRUE CHRISTIAN HAVE A DEMON?

The Popular Belief

Praise the LORD, Dear Hearts! I decided to do this message due to a comment I received on my Facebook post. A young lady commented, "A true Christian cannot have a demon within, demons only attack them from the outside, but never from within." Dear Hearts, I know that's the popular belief and that's what has been taught; but can a Christian have a demon? The answer is yes. Some people may say, "Well, if they have a demon that means they are not a true Christian."

Am I a True Christian?

Dear Hearts, there are many true Christians that have demons. They have demons living in their mind, their will, their emotions and their body. Why? Because of their lack of knowing TRUTH. Remember, when we come to the LORD, we are babes in Christ Jesus. It's our spirit that is birthed into the family of God by the Holy Spirit (John 3:6) and our spirit is off limits to the enemy, Satan and his cohorts. Even though the enemy cannot change our new birth in the Family of God, we must realize our body is still on earth and we have the same soul, which is the mind, will and emotions. These areas are not new. They need to be renewed day-by-day (Romans 12:2) according to the Word of God by his Spirit. God's Word teaches us how to walk by the Spirit (Galatians 5:16) so we can stay free.

Why did Christ Jesus give deliverance to us? It's because of our disobedience and lack of knowing (or knowledge). Now, does that mean just because we're Christians, a follower and learner of Jesus Christ and have demons living in the mind, will, emotions and/or body that we're not TRUE Christians? No, it does not mean that. Demons love to hide in darkness and not be exposed because they know once they're exposed, they have to leave (Mark 3:27). It just means that we need to be delivered. Dear Hearts, It was just Jesus' grace and mercy in the way he orchestrated in leading me to be free. I had received the Baptism of the Holy Spirit with the evidence of speaking in tongues. It was about a month after that the LORD let me know that a demon was living within. So, yes! You do have some true Christians who are tongue talkers that have demons. Now again, does that make the person false? No, they're just deceived. They're living in a lack of knowing. A lack of knowledge of God's Word, but as they continue to pursue the LORD with all their heart, the LORD says, "When you seek me with all your heart then I will allow you to find me (Jeremiah 29:13)."

Dear Hearts, Jesus looked at me and saw that I was seeking him with my whole heart. I desired nobody but him and he was not going to leave me in that condition. He looked down upon me and saw filthiness in my mind, in my will, in my emotions and in my body that I was clueless of and he set me free. It was just his grace and mercy; but the point is, I pursued him. I did everything within my power not to disobey him and he had mercy upon me (1 John 1:9). Dear Hearts, again can a Christian have a demon? Yes and some of you may think, "The demon is really harassing me from the outside. They cannot on the inside." Yes, they can. If you have never been delivered and are not staying obedient and submitting to God's Word (James 4:7); then yes, a true Christian can have a demon. Now, if you're one of them that says, "Well, I don't believe that." It's proof that demons are living in your soul in getting you to disbelieve the Word of God.

Dear Hearts, who do you think the apostles were speaking to? They always spoke to the church, to true Christians. If you read the book of Ephesians, Galatians, Corinthians, the Apostle Paul spoke the Word of God in correction to Christians. Especially the Galatians, the Apostle Paul told the true Christians not to be involved in the works of the flesh because they were doing those things (Galatians 5:19-21). They were failing to be in submission to God. Again, did that make them false and not true Christians? No, they were true Christians, but they were deceived. They were probably like some of you who think they could not have demons because of being born again and speaking in tongues.

Dear Hearts, Christians can have demons living in their mind, will, emotions and body because of their disobedience to God's Word and failing to remain in submission to God. Yes, a true Christian can have demons and demons know that. They know that their only legal right to God's child is sin, wrongdoings and disobedience. The point is, just because a demon may be living in us doesn't mean we are not true Christians? REMEMBER, a Christian is a person who is truly learning and following the LORD and desiring and loving him with all their heart. We are true Christians. We're just deceived. Jesus said, "My people are destroyed because of lack of knowledge (Hosea 4:6)". Even though we are in God's Word and learning his Word, there are areas we are deceived in and we don't have knowledge in; demons take advantage of our lack of knowing. Praise the living God!

What is Sin?

The Scriptures says, "All wrongdoings is sin (1 John 5:17) and even knowing to do good and do it not (James 4:17)." God is telling us to do good and we still won't do it. That's what happened to King Saul (1 Samuel 15th Chapter). The LORD kept telling him to do good and he would not do it. He partially did it. Yes, that will open the door for one to become demonized whether they're a true Christian or not. Yes, true Christians can be demonized. We must live in submission to God. Even the LORD said that whenever we don't receive of him by faith that is sin (Romans 14:23). We have to be careful even with that. Dear Hearts, we just need to stay humble before the LORD and just say, "LORD, only you can keep me, only you can keep me." Make it a daily prayer in saying, "Search my heart. If you, LORD, find any unclean thing in me, rid it out of me (Psalm 139:23-24)." Our problem is we can't find anything wrong with us. Dear Hearts, I thank God he didn't leave it up to me to find anything wrong with me because I wouldn't have been able to see it. I didn't know it. I didn't see when that demon entered me. When we hear a Christian say, "A Christian cannot have demons," we should ask, "In whose eyes are you looking through when you say that? Are you basing it on what you see?" Dear Hearts, let a true Christian continue to walk in and live by disobedience; I guarantee, that disobedience will be attached with a demon. Praise the living God!

Delegated Authority

Now, once a person becomes a Christian; and let's define Christian, a Christian is a follower and learner of Jesus, the Christ. Do you not know there are many Christians, even after coming to the LORD that are not being taught or disciple to Christ Jesus? Most ministers disciple people to their church or organization and not to Christ Jesus. Because of that, many true Christians have become demonized. They've never been set free. The demons within their mind, their will, emotions, and body had never been confronted and commanded to leave God's house (1 Corinthians 6:19).

God delegated that authority to us, human beings, who have the Spirit of God in them and walking and living by the Holy Spirit's leadership (Luke 10:19). Before the LORD went to sit at the right hand of His Heavenly Father, he gave gifts to mankind; and one of those gifts He said, "In my name, you shall ..." Shall do what? You shall cast out devils (Mark 16:17). He wasn't talking about casting out devils from people who were living in the world. He was talking about casting them out of His own; for deliverance is the children's bread (Matthew 15:26). Again, God has delegated authority to human beings, those who have accepted him and walking by his Spirit, to cast demon spirits out of a person's mind, will, emotions and body.

Rebellion is Witchcraft

You know, some of you are saying, "No, Christians can't have demons." But look at you, woman (of God)! You're not submitted to your husband as he submits to the LORD (Ephesians 5:22). You always tell him what to do. You refuse to even listen. As a matter of fact, you don't even listen to your pastor as he submits to the LORD (Hebrews 13:17). And yet; you say, "A Christian cannot have a demon." Your behavior shows your husband, pastor and you there are demons of rebellion living in your mind, will, emotions and body. The Scripture says, "Rebellion is as the sin of witchcraft (1 Samuel 15:23). Therefore; some Christian women are operating in witchcraft. A demon spirit Jezebel can be found living there as well. Praise the living God! We need to humble ourselves, Dear Hearts. Humble ourselves before the LORD (James 4:10) and say, "LORD, keep me by your Spirit (Psalm 16:1) and help me to allow you to keep me. Help me not to stray away from you."

When we pray Deuteronomy 31:6, "Jesus, don't leave me and forsake me"; we should also pray, "Jesus help me. Don't let me leave you or forsake you because I know you will never leave and forsake me. Jesus, clean me up." We need to be like His servant, David. That's why he loved David, a man after His own heart. David was full of wisdom and the Word of God through Psalms and Proverbs tells us so. Even his son, Solomon tells how his dad was full of wisdom. That's why Solomon was blessed with wisdom because of his father. But yet and still, David kept himself low and humble. He belittled himself and said, "Jesus, help me. Search my heart. You know everything. You see everything. If there is any darkness in my mind, will, emotions and body; Jesus, I ask you to rid it out of me. Clean me and wash me by your Blood. You know everything. (Psalm 139:23)." We need to keep ourselves humble in asking the LORD and not go around saying, "I don't believe what Evangelist King says because a true Christian cannot have demons." Its proof that such rebellious attitude is evidence there are demon spirits living within! Praise the living God!

Submissive to God

Dear Hearts, we need to be submitted to God according to James 4:7. Just because we are a true Christian doesn't mean we cannot have demons. The only way demons cannot be in a Christian and live and dwell within them is because the Christian is living in obedience to God according to James 4:7, which is, "Submitting to God." In every area of our life we should SUBMIT to God and then we'll be in a position to RESIST the devil and devils will FLEE from us. Here the LORD is telling us if we don't submit to him, then we're not going to resist the devil and he's not going to flee from us. He's going to jump into our mind, will, emotions, and body. Again, as a true Christian, a believer in Christ Jesus, born again and birthed by his Spirit, devils cannot jump into our spirit. He cannot control our spirit, but I want you to remember the LORD said, "The soul that sins, it shall die (Ezekiel 18:20)." What's the soul? It's the mind, the will and the emotions. Therefore; when we sin in those areas, the LORD said we shall die. Praise the living God!

Dear Hearts, we should stop believing true Christians cannot have demons because they are true Christians. That's not the reason why true Christians don't have demons. The reason true Christians cannot have demons is because they are submitting to the authority and the obedience of God; and by submitting to God, we're able to resist the devil and the devil will flee from us. Submission to God is what causes us not to invite demons to come and dwell in God's house, which is our mind, will, emotions and body. Praise the living God! Dear Hearts, don't let Satan deceive you! He has subtle traps. That's the reason why we need to get understanding of God's Word through his Spirit. Many people get understanding through the teachings of mankind by searching the internet. No! You have to listen to the Spirit of God (John 16:13). When you listen to people over the internet, you ask the Holy Spirit, "Holy Spirit, as I'm listening to Evangelist King, take me to your Word. Prove this to me by your Word." Praise the living God!

My Damascus Experience

I know these things because of the Word of God and also because of my own experience. If you're going to talk about certain things, include yourself? Talk about yourself. Stop talking about somebody else. When I first gave my heart to the LORD, I gave him my all. I was truly a follower and learner of Christ Jesus. I did not know that a demon was living in my mind, will, emotions and body. I was clueless in knowing this truth. If someone would have told me that I was demonized, I would have looked look at them and said, "You're a liar! I'm a child of God!" Dear Hearts, demons were there. It was just Jesus' grace and mercy that set me FREE.

The Apostle Paul had a Damascus Experience, described in Paul's own words in Acts 9:1–9; Acts 22:6–11; and Acts 26:9–20. I know about my Damascus Experience. I loved the LORD. I worshiped him; but Dear Heart, I did not know that a demon was in me. There was some type of evidence, but the demon even had me to overlook it and not dwell on it and that's what demons do when they are in you. They force you to say words to people and you don't remember saying it at the time. You'll say, "I didn't say that. I didn't do that." Dear Hearts, that's a clue a demon is in the house. Because when demons are in you; they come up and blank you out. You don't remember what you said. You don't know what you did. I remember once with my husband and family. We were eating with my parents and talking. All of a sudden I blanked out and when I came through everybody was looking at me and I was wondering, "Why are they looking at me." At that moment, I couldn't remember what happened. I thought to myself, I must've said something that really wasn't good because the way my stepfather looked at me. When I looked at him I said to myself, "I knew he wouldn't just look at me like that. I must've said something." Dear Hearts, I was too afraid to even ask, "What did I just say?" because I was afraid to know what it was. Right then the LORD was giving me a hint, "Terry, there's something wrong with you," but that demon in me suppressed that and did not allow me to think about it any further.

Dear Hearts, I thank Jesus for his grace and mercy. He didn't give up on me. I remember one time I was in my meditation time with him, just having a conversation with him. Just think, Dear Hearts, we have a conversation with Jesus and he looks and sees everything. He sees in the mind. He sees in the will. He sees in the emotions. He sees in the body. He sees in the spirit. He sees everything (Hebrews 4:13). When you look at me you just see my body. That's all you can see, but Jesus sees everything, and he's talking to me and saw there was darkness in me and he talked to me. Some of you are not like that. If you know something is wrong with Evangelist King, you won't even call, sit and/or talk with me. "You say, "I'm not talking to Evangelist King. She's not right. I'm not going to listen to her." Dear Hearts, I'm so glad Jesus doesn't have that type of attitude. That type of attitude is not of Jesus Christ; and yes, you have a demon with such attitude. Praise the living God! Thank you Jesus, glory to your Holy name. Jesus will talk to me anyway. That's who he is, grace and mercy. The good thing is that he doesn't allow us to stay that way when we call out to him (Jeremiah 33:3).

Jesus says in Galatian 6:1, "Brothers, suppose someone is caught doing something wrong..." See, I was doing things wrong and that darkness was in me and Jesus knew it. He continues to say, "...You who have the Spirit should set him right..." Jesus, who is the Spirit, set me right. We're supposed to set the same example as Jesus. We see our brother or sister do wrong, they are Christian, they are wrong, they are in deception. The LORD said, "We who have the Spirit of God in us, we should set them right." Why, because that's what Jesus did. That's who Jesus is. He said, "We should set them right, but in a spirit of humility, keeping an eye on ourselves so that we won't be tempted too." That's how Jesus did me, in the spirit of humility because that's who he is, he set me right. He told you and me to keep an eye on ourselves so that we won't be tempted to sin. Praise the living God! Dear Hearts, the same grace and mercy Jesus showed us, we're supposed to show one another. Right now, I'm doing this message because the same grace and mercy he showed me, I'm showing you. Jesus looked on me and saw that darkness in me and he set me right. He didn't say, "I'm not having anything to do with that woman with that darkness in her." His grace and mercy took me in and he refused to allow me to remain in darkness and set me right.

I remember this one day in my meditation time with him, he said, "Terry." I said, "Yes, LORD." Yes, Dear Hearts, Jesus will talk with you. Spend time with him and you will see he will talk to you. He said, "I want you to go to the women's prayer breakfast." At that time my husband found out about this women's prayer breakfast and told me about it. I never felt led to go, not until the LORD said, "I want you to go." I said, "Yes, LORD." He gave me specific instructions. When Jesus gives you specific instructions, Dear Hearts, you need to follow every precept and line. He said, "When you go, I want you to stand up when worship starts. It doesn't matter if you're the only one standing or not. I want you to stand up and hold up your hands and worship me." I said, "Yes, LORD." He also said, "I'm going to send the woman of God to you and she's going to lay her hands on you." I then asked my husband. I said, "Roger, when the women's prayer breakfast come up this week, could you take me?" He said, "Yes." He took me. When worship began, I stood up and held my hands up and began to worship the LORD in spirit and in truth. My eyes were closed. Dear Hearts, as I worshipped him, I saw in the spirit realm the woman of God coming to me. I knew it was the LORD Jesus letting me know what was going on in the spirit realm even though it was the woman who was coming to me in the physical realm. Remember Jesus said we are his body. When you have the Spirit of God in you, you are his body (1 Corinthians 3:16). As she did, who is God's body, Christ Jesus did.

Then she began to speak words in my ears, even though that was her speaking words in my ears, Dear Hearts, I heard Jesus. Jesus was literally talking through her. Jesus only did what she did. She only did what Jesus would have her to do. That's why we should stop looking at gender, race and we should even stop looking at the human being and see Jesus and hear Jesus through the person. As Jesus was speaking, I was listening to him with all my might and something was preventing me from clearly hearing him. I remember asking Jesus, "Could you speak up because I can hardly hear you?" I was trying to hear him with all my might and something was still blocking me from clearly hearing him. I then said to myself, "What is this that is blocking me from hearing him clearly?" But Jesus kept talking and I did hear what he said and I thanked him. Then I saw, in the spirit, Jesus through the woman and the woman's hand. She put her hand at my belly. She didn't put it on my belly. When she did, something in my belly came to the attention of her hand and I said to myself, "What is that? What is that in my belly?" I saw her hand as it gradually moved upward. Whatever that was in my belly was moving upward as her hand moved upward and my mind was saying, "What is this coming up in my belly? What is going on?" My spirit was trying to hear what Jesus was saying. Dear Hearts, you are a spirit. You have a soul, mind, and will, emotions and you have a body for this earth. At that moment, I experienced all three portions of the human man; spirit, soul, and body. Here, again, as she gradually moved her hand up and something was coming up with her hand. Then I noticed her hand stopped and whatever was in my belly stopped. Praise the living God! LORD, we thank you for your mighty power of the Holy Ghost!

The LORD said, "I am with you (Matthew 28:20)." I am working with you. God was working with that lady because he was in her. Praise the living God! She moved her hand upward again and whatever was in my belly moved upward. She got her hand up to my mouth and the thing stopped right at my mouth. In the spirit realm, I felt and saw when she waved her hand like you wave something goodbye. When she did that, she said, "There it goes!" I remember my eyes were closed, so when she said, "There it goes!" I felt something fly out of my mouth. I literally felt when it flew out of my mouth and immediately my spirit knew what was going on while my mind was clueless. My mind was clueless but my spirit knew, so immediately my spirit, from my belly, said, "Thank you, Jesus!" really quick and rapidly. "Thank you Jesus, thank you Jesus, thank you Jesus," but my mind was saying, "Why am I saying thank you Jesus? What was it that flew out of my mouth?" The LORD gave me this experience, Dear Hearts, for his reason. I have come to see it's because he wanted me in the future to share with you who say Christians cannot have demons.

Again, my spirit knew what was happening, but my mind was clueless and said, "Why am I saying thank you Jesus? What flew out of my mouth? Something flew out of my mouth!" Later on when I went home and got back into my meditation room in the area where I just meditated on the things of God, the Holy Spirit brought that whole incident back to mind. Remember, my mind was clueless about what was going on, but my spirit was so happy, and I did feel free and light. I felt good. So I finally said, "Oh yeah, LORD, something flew out of my mouth. What was that?" Dear Hearts, you can talk to the LORD just like you talk to a human person. Just be yourself. Don't try to go before him religious. So I asked him, "LORD, something flew out of my mouth. What was it?" He said, "Terry, it was a demon." When the LORD said "a demon," I said, "What! A demon? What right did a demon have in me?" The LORD said, "You remember what the Holy Spirit has been telling you? When he said that, Dear Hearts, I dropped my head and repented.

I was not in obedience to God. I was not in submission to him; and because of that, it opened the door for that demon to enter me through my mouth down into my belly through my disobedience. The disobedience was that I failed to exercise self-control. Remember one of the fruits of the Holy Spirit is self-control (Galatians 5:22-23). At that time, Dear Hearts, I loved Coca-Cola. Now, there's nothing wrong with drinking Coca-Cola. That wasn't the problem. The problem was I did not exercise self-control. I drank so many liters of Coke a day. I just had to have a Coke. It was something I had to have. Like some of you, you have to have your caffeine, your coffee or whatever, see, that's a false comfort and the Holy Spirit was warning me about false comfort. He said, "Terry, you need to stop that. You need to stop drinking so many Cokes. You need to control yourself." He was telling me that. I heard him, but I did not obey him, but I kept on and on and on. I didn't know when it entered me. It entered me through that disobedience in failing to submit to God. Yes, Dear Hearts, a Christian can have demons; and because of God's grace and mercy, he set me free. Praise the living God!

Your Helper

I pray that the LORD will lead you to your helper. First of all, you have to humble yourself and admit to the LORD, "I don't know everything. I cannot see everything. LORD, you know everything and I ask you to look in me and if you see any unclean thing, rid me of it. Lead me to my helper." Stop trying to cast demons out of yourself. How can you cast something out that you can't even see? You don't even know it's there. I couldn't cast something out of me that I didn't know that was even in me. The LORD said, I needed a helper. We need a helper, Dear Hearts. We need one another. We need each other. Praise the living God! The main thing is to keep ourselves low and humble. Demons are defiant. They refuse to submit and humble themselves before God, and if you happen to be listening and you don't want to humble yourself or even to admit that a Christian can have a demon that shows defiance is in you, and yes, you have a demon. You need to be delivered, so ask God to send you to your helper. Praise the living God!

PESTERING FAITH

What is Pestering Faith?

Dear Hearts, another word for faith is trust. There are many kinds of faith and the Holy Spirit reveals to us the different levels. This particular faith is found in the Word of God known as pestering faith (Matthew 15:21-28). Pestering faith is very important. It doesn't give up, no matter what. No matter how much you say it's secondary or not important, pestering faith doesn't give up. Pestering faith is a faith that will harass God. It doesn't give up or give in. The word 'pester' means 'one that harass with petty irritation'. The word 'petty' means 'secondary rank or importance', so when something is petty you don't consider it to be important. You put it on the back burner. With the Canaanite woman, her faith was considered to be a pestering faith because she was not an Israelite, but a Canaanite and Jesus reminded her that he was only sent to the lost sheep of the house of Israel. Her faith was considered to be a pestering faith. It wasn't important and Jesus told her that to continue to test her faith. The Scripture indicates to us that she had a pestering faith. She needed the Lord to set her daughter free from demons that were cruelly attacking her. She had pestering faith, the type of faith God wants us to have.

There comes a time we should have pestering faith that doesn't give up. No matter what a person may think of us or feel we're not important. Regardless of how much a person may say we're irritating, irritable or harassing them. It doesn't matter, we need pestering faith. Jesus Christ love pestering faith. Human beings may get upset with us when we pester them, for example, when we want something from them and they keep saying no, but we keep asking; and after a while; they'll say, "You're getting on my nerves. Leave me." Human beings may say we're irritable or not important, but not Jesus Christ. Jesus Christ would never think or say such a thing; for he loves pestering faith. Praise the living God!

How to Pray?

Before we can have pestering faith, we must know how to pray and what to pray. Christ Jesus through his disciples, taught us how to pray and what to pray. He taught that we should pray TRUTH. What is truth? God's Word is truth. Jesus said, "I AM the Way and the Truth and the Life; no one comes to the Father except through me." Therefore, before we can KEEP asking, KEEP seeking and KEEP knocking; we must first know how to pray. Jesus wants us to pray truth, so we must be careful in what we pray. We should pray how Jesus prayed, which is God's Word. Remember, faith (or trust) in God comes by hearing and hearing the Word of God (Romans 10:17).

The first step to praying is to confess God as our Heavenly Father and that His name is holy; for he will not leave unpunished someone who uses his name lightly (Exodus 20:7). We are to confess his kingdom through his Son, Jesus Christ (Matthew 3:2). Luke 11:1-4 says, "One time Jesus was in a certain place praying. As he finished, one of the disciples said to him, "Sir, teach us to pray, just as John taught his disciples." He said to them, "When you pray, say: 'Father, May your name be kept holy. May your Kingdom come. Give us each day the food we need. Forgive us our sins, for we too forgive everyone who has wronged us. And do not lead us to hard testing.'"

Dear Hearts, we're to pray and ask the Lord to fill our every need according to his glorious wealth, in union with the Christ Jesus (Philippians 4:19). It is God the Father through Jesus Christ by the Holy Spirit that each day he feeds and clothes us. We are to forgive those who have harmed and wronged us. Just as we have wronged and harmed our Heavenly Father and he has forgiven us, we are to forgive those who have done us wrong. Then we are to pray that the Father does not lead us to hard testing. If the Father leads us to hard testing, dear hearts, we will not get out of it. Each person is being tempted whenever they are being dragged off and enticed by the bait of their own desire (James 1:14). Would we tempt our children with evil? No, we would not. But if evil is in us, then we're going to go towards that evil, so Jesus told us to pray. It is the Tempter, Satan, who tries to get us to rebel and sin against God through hard testing (Matthew 4:3).

Often times our prayers are not answered because we ask outside the will of God. We don't receive because we pray with the wrong motive that of wanting to indulge our own desires (James 4:3). We must stay in God's will. Whatever we're trusting and believing the LORD for, we should first find out if it's his will or in his Word. If it's his will or in his Word, then we should go ahead and pray to remind him of his will or Word. Then we shall receive. Praise the living God!

PESTERING Faith Keep Asking

Luke 11:5-8 says, "He also said to them, "Suppose one of you has a friend; and you go to him in the middle of the night and say to him, 'Friend, lend me three loaves of bread, because a friend of mine who has been travelling has just arrived at my house, and I have nothing for him to eat.' Now the one inside may answer, 'Don't bother me! The door is already shut, my children are with me in bed - I can't get up to give you anything!' But I tell you, even if he won't get up because the man is his friend, yet because of the man's hutzpah (shameless audacity) he will get up and give him as much as he needs." When we're truly in need, we don't give up. We just keep on pestering the person in asking until we receive help. That's a shameless audacity! We're not ashamed of being in need. We're not ashamed to ask for help. The shame is when we are full of pride and will not humble ourselves in asking for help. Therefore, before we can even ask and receive of God, we MUST be humble in spirit (James 4:6). God opposes the proud and arrogant. We need to be humble; and if we're not, we need to ask the Lord to humble us. For he perceives the proud from afar (Psalm 138:6). When we're truly in need, we just don't care how we may look or sound in asking for help. All we want is for our friend to help us.

Luke 11:9-10 says, "Moreover, I myself say to you: keep asking, and it will be given to you; keep seeking, and you will find; keep knocking, and the door will be opened to you. For everyone who goes on asking receives; and he who goes on seeking finds; and to him who continues knocking, the door will be opened." The Lord is saying not to give up. He said to keep asking. Does that mean I keep asking him the same thing over and over again? No. When we ask, we ask in faith. We ask believing. The Lord is teaching us not go give up on believing or trusting. No matter how long in the natural realm for things to manifest, we don't give up. He said to keep asking and then it will be given to us. So if I ask you and you give it to me, then I don't need to ask you anymore because I already have it. So what the LORD is actually saying is, "Don't give up!" Keep trusting!

PESTERING Faith Keep Seeking

We asked and received. Now Jesus Christ is instructing us to keep seeking. We should keep seeking with all our heart. Then we shall find. He is still saying we should not give up. Whatever we're believing and trusting God for, we don't give up. We should keep asking and keep seeking, which means keep believing that we have received. Everyone who goes on asking, receives. Everyone who goes on seeking, finds. Therefore, when we ask and it have not manifested in the natural realm, don't have an attitude that gives up! Don't stop trusting (asking)! Don't stop seeking! When we go on seeking, the Lord says we shall find provided we seek him wholeheartedly (Jeremiah 29:13). Just as when we didn't stop until we found our spouse. We kept seeking until we found them. After finding our spouse, some wish they had never found them. Dear Hearts, we will never get it wrong with Christ Jesus. His heart is like a flashlight. It searches (or seeks) our heart for any darkness; and if it's there, his Spirit drives it out. It's his desire to keep us from ALL darkness (Matthew 6:13). So we should keep seeking and we shall find when we seek him with our whole heart.

PESTERING Faith Keep Knocking

Luke 11:11-13 says, "Is there any father here who, if his son asked him for a fish, would instead of a fish give him a snake? Or if he asked for an egg would give him a scorpion? So if you, even though you are bad, know how to give your children gifts that are good, how much more will the Father keep giving the Holy Spirit from heaven to those who keep asking him!" Dear Hearts, we'll never get it wrong with Jesus Christ. He said to never stop seeking, never stop asking and never stop knocking. For EVERYONE who goes on asking, receives; seeking, finds; and knocking, door opens. That means, "WE GOT IT!" God is not going to withhold the Holy Spirit from us. It's his desire that we enter into the fullness of the Holy Spirit. It is his desire that we form a relationship with the Holy Spirit. The Holy Spirit is in us, but he also wants to come upon us. He wants to come upon us to do the Father's will through Jesus Christ to bring glory to his name on earth. That's why we should keep trusting, keep asking and keep knocking. We shouldn't give up. We should believe we have already received and thank him for his goodness and mercy. For everyone who goes on knocking, the door opens. Dear Hearts, pestering faith NEVER stop asking, seeking and knocking! Praise the living God!

The Canaanite Woman

Matthew 15:21-28 says, "Jesus left that place and went off to Tyre and Sidon. A woman from Canaan, who was living there, came to him, pleading." Dear Hearts, in regard to the works that Jesus did, she heard about him. She heard how he set captives free, healed the sick and opened blinded eyes. She heard the great miracles of Jesus Christ. She heard those things and one day Jesus came to her home town. Dear Hearts, when God sends a man or woman of God which is His servant to your hometown, it's best you make your way out and be in the midst of God's servant, because Jesus Christ sent his servant for a purpose, which is to set you free. You need pestering faith. Faith that doesn't give up. I guarantee you the Canaanite woman, when Jesus came to her town, the devil put obstacles in her way; but because she had pestering faith, she did not allow the enemy's obstacles to stop her from going out and seeing the man of God. You and I must be the same way, Dear Hearts.

Again, it says that Jesus came to her home town and she came to him pleading. She came to Jesus pleading and asking. She was pestering him because she was in need. Dear Hearts, she wasn't concerned whether she bothered him or not. She didn't say, "Excuse me, Lord, I really hate pestering you." No, she did not. She was pleading with him because when you are need you are in need. This woman was in need. She said, "Sir, have pity on me. Son of David, my daughter is cruelly held under the power of demons." This woman was suffering and seeing her beautiful daughter being tormented on the inside with demons causing her daughter to hurt herself. I believe those demons spoke through her daughter and poked fun at the mother so that she knew they held her daughter captive. Can you imagine what this woman was going through? Dear Hearts, she probably shared with her neighbors and friends what these demons said and how they acted through her daughter and they did not believe her.

Dear Hearts, she heard that Jesus casted devils out of people. She heard about the young man who was in Gadara possessed with demons and Jesus set him free (Mark 5:1-20). She heard things concerning the works that Jesus did and she saw the enemy had her daughter, so when Jesus came to her home town, she did not allow the enemies' hindrances and blockages to stop her from going to the man of God and pestering him for help. She came to him with a humble spirit. She pestered him because of being in need. She said, "Sir, have pity on me." Some of us, we're so proud we don't want anybody to have pity on us. Dear Hearts, God can put us in a situation that we have no other choice but to ask someone to have pity on us. Pestering faith is a humble type of faith that is not concerned about its reputation. That's the reason why a lot of us need deliverance from demons within; and because of our reputation, we do not want to go where God sends his servant in our home town. We allow our reputation to stop us. Dear Hearts, it's best to go and get delivered now than go to hell along with your reputation burning in the hell's fire and demons tormenting you and you're in hell crying, "Lord, I should have went to the Holy Ghost FIRE Deliverance Meeting that you were holding with your servant Evangelist King. I should have went. I should have gotten set free!" Dear Hearts, it will be too late then.

Dear Hearts, pestering faith is a harassment with petty irritations; but in the eyes of God, it's not petty. Praise the living God! Again, the Canaan woman asked the Lord, "Have mercy on me, son of David. My daughter is cruelly held under the power of demons." The demons were really afflicting her daughter and causing her to harm herself. The demons were beating, leaving bruises and bite marks on her daughter's body. Dear Hearts, here's a mother watching her beautiful child being tormented. You may ask, "How did her daughter get demonized?" Because the daughter, through disobedience, dabbed her hand into witchcraft and by doing so, she became demon possessed. Dear Hearts, we can teach our children to do the right thing, but it's up to them to do what is right. When her daughter dabbed her hand in witchcraft, she opened a door for demons to enter, attack and torment her. Praise the Lord! The mother had pestering faith. Faith that did not give up. Faith that pesters the Lord. Faith that says, "Lord, I'm not going to give up. I'm coming to you. Have mercy on me. Have pity upon me, Lord."

I want you to pay special attention to how Jesus handled the Canaanite woman's request. Dear Hearts, Jesus will test us. When we ask the Lord for something and he doesn't immediately do it, this is when pestering faith needs to kick in because Jesus is testing us to see if we truly are going to continue believing him in knocking and asking (Luke 11:9-13). The verse says, "But Jesus did not say a word to her..." Here's this woman with pestering faith. She was pestering Jesus. She was irritating and walking along with them crying, "Son of David, have mercy on me! Have pity on me!" The way she was crying, I guarantee you she wasn't saying it in a calm voice. She was crying with an irritable sound. She was pleading for help. She was in agony and pain. She needed Him to help her and she continued to ask Him for pity and mercy through that agony in her heart and it was irritating; very irritating. Praise the Lord! It was an irritable sound, but not to Jesus. To the human ears, it may sound irritable; but to the spiritual ears, it's a lovely and beautiful sound to the Lord. Praise the Lord!

In the natural realm, Jesus doesn't say a word. Why? Because he'll test us. Some of you, right now, have asked the Lord to set you free, just like Paul, from a particular matter and only you know what that is. In other words, it's your thorn in the flesh; and just like Paul, you're pleading with the Lord to take it away. Just as with the Canaanite woman, the Lord is not saying a word. This is where you need pestering faith. Keep pestering him by asking and knocking. No matter how it irritates the human ears. I get secondary and third deliverance requests from certain individuals; but every now and then, it'll be one, two or three people and especially this one person who sends a note requesting deliverance every year. I received another deliverance request and the first thing the person said, "It's not my desire that I should be any burden to you." As I was reading it, I thought, "Jesus is in me and they're not irritating." I also heard Jesus say, "Don't say a word." Then there are times when the Lord says, "Speak to the person and tell them thus says the Lord." The majority of the time, the Lord says, "Don't say a word." Now, I truly understand the Lord's reason for doing that. He is testing the person's faith. It's good for the person to have pestering faith. They have not given up on God regardless of how the Lord choose not to say a word. The person still continues to ask of the Lord and question certain things because they have pestering faith and that's good. By the way, if you happen to hear this message, you know who I'm referring to. It's good what you're doing. The Lord wants you to know it's called pestering faith. You are not pestering God and neither are you pestering his servant. That is a sweet sound to God's ears because it proves to him that you are not giving up.

Verse 23 continues to say, "But Jesus did not say a word to her. Then his disciples came to him and urged him..." Now, his disciples were right there hearing and seeing this woman. To them, she was really an irritation. She irritated them. Why? Because the disciples at that moment were not converted. They were not converted until Jesus died, rose again, came through the wall and appeared to them and the Scripture said Jesus breathed on them. When Jesus breathed on them, the Holy Spirit entered and they were converted or born again (John 20:22). They then acted differently than before. They no longer were led by their mind. Before they were in competition with one another. They wanted God to harm people whenever they did not listen and receive Jesus. Two of them even said, "Let's call down fire, Lord, and burn them all, they don't want to hear you (Luke 9:54)." The disciples were led by their carnal mind or way of thinking. So they said to Jesus, "Send her away, because she is following us and keeps pestering us with her crying." To the carnal mind or way of thinking, pestering faith sounds irritating; but to the spiritual minded, it's a sweet sound. When a person has pestering faith and you are walking by a carnal mind, the sound will be irritating to you. As the unconverted disciples, you'll say, "Get away! Go away! Don't call me anymore! I don't want to have anything else to do with you! You're irritating! You're pestering me!" Remember, the woman wasn't following the disciples. She was following Jesus. That's how the carnal mind thinks, "She's following us and keeps pestering us with her crying." Dear Hearts, if you've got to cry, you cry to Jesus. Have pestering faith. Faith that doesn't give up. Don't give up because it's a sweet sound to Jesus' ears.

Dear Hearts, notice the Scripture says Jesus didn't say a word to her; but when his disciples spoke, he then spoke to the woman because he did not want her to get discouraged because of what his disciples said. When unbelief and doubt is about to attack us due to hearing what someone, especially of high standards, says that's contrary to his word, Jesus will send his Spirit to correct us because he doesn't want us to lose faith in him. Just think! His disciples, who are with him, spoke discouraging words and the woman heard them, it would have caused her to lose hope and faith in the Lord. Jesus was about to let her know not to rely on his unconverted disciples, but to keep her eyes and faith on him. This is where he continues to test the woman to see she if she has pestering faith. Faith that doesn't give up. Faith that doesn't give in. He turned to the woman and said, "I was only sent to the lost sheep of the house of Israel." This was a Canaanite woman. She was not Jewish and was not considered to be part of Israel, but an outcast, a sinner, a Canaanite. The Lord reminded her of that. Remember, he said it to test her faith. God allows certain things to happen to us and will allow certain people to say certain things to us to test our faith to see if we will continue to have pestering faith.

When Jesus told the woman he was sent only to the lost sheep of the house of Israel, she didn't stop pestering him. Verse 25 says, "But she came, fell at his feet and said, "Sir, help me!" Now, that's pestering faith! Faith that doesn't give up and is not concerned about what may be said. It doesn't matter. Faith that says I hear what you say and I don't hear what you say. I'm going to continue to pester God in helping me. I'll continue to fall on my knees and be humble. It doesn't matter what you think of me. It doesn't matter what you say of me, I'm going to continue to have pestering faith. I'm going to pester God until he answers my request. That's what the Canaanite woman did. Verse 26 says, "He answered..." Here Jesus again still testing the woman to see if she's going to give up on her pestering faith. He continues to say, "...It is not right to take the children's food and toss it to their pet dogs." Deliverance is the children's bread (or food).

Now, some of us, if Jesus would call us a dog through his servant, we would turn around and walk away. Wouldn't we? We would shout, "You're calling me a dog! Forget it!" Dear Hearts, pestering faith doesn't think or act contrary to how the Holy Spirit wants us to be. The Canaanite woman didn't think contrary. Jesus did refer to the woman as a dog. When I first read this story when I was a teenager, I said, "Jesus, you're calling her a dog!" But now I know, he was testing her because of her pestering faith-a faith that harasses no matter if you look on me as being secondary in need or secondary importance-no matter if you look on me as if my request is irritating you. I'm going to pester you, Jesus, until you give me what I want. Remember, pestering faith is a sweet sound to the ears of God, because pestering faith doesn't give up. Pestering faith keeps believing and trusting God.

After the Lord told the woman it's not right to take the children's bread and toss it to their pet dogs; with humility and humbleness of heart, she said, "This is true, sir..." Dear Hearts, the Holy Spirit was the person who inspired the woman to say these words to Jesus. She replied, "...but even the dogs eat the leftovers that fall from their master's table." Praise the living God! I was a little girl when I read that and I shouted for joy. I said, "Lord, that was the Holy Ghost who revealed that to her." In other words, she said, "Yes, even the dogs eat the leftovers. True, Lord, I might not be the lost sheep of the house of Israel, but those leftovers that they have carelessly dropped and rejected, I'll take those. I'll take the leftovers." Because of what she said in her pestering faith; verse 28 says, "Then Jesus answered her, 'Lady, you are a person of great trust. Let your desire be granted.' And her daughter was healed at that very moment." Those demons easily entered into her daughter because of the lack of faith of the mother. Jesus allowed her faith to be tested so that it would increase and grow deeper into her heart. Because her trust was so great, she passed the tests. The Lord credited her faith to great trust; and at that very moment, her daughter was delivered.

Again, parents; your child's deliverance is tied up in your obedience to God. Do you trust God? Do you have pestering faith? Faith, that pesters God and continues to ask and believe that He will do his will as you have reminded Him, because it is His will that your child be set free, for you to be set free, for your family to be set free. Don't give up and no matter what the circumstances are, don't give in. Continue with pestering faith. Jesus loves it when we pester him. It's a sweet sound to his hearing. To carnal minded man, it's an irritable sound to their ears; but to Jesus, it's a sweet sound to his ears. No matter what people may say, be as the Canaanite woman, continue in pestering faith. Even Jacob had pestering faith. He wrestled with the angel all night long until he got blessed. He said to the angel, "I'm not letting you go until you bless me." Now, that's pestering faith! Praise the living God! The angel threw Jacob's hip bone out of place so that he could turn him loose, but Jacob still did not stop until he was blessed. Dear Hearts, that's what you and I need to have is pestering faith. It doesn't matter if a person, whether man or woman, even if they're a child of God say you're pestering them. Say, "I'm not pestering anyone, but God!" Praise the living God!

Prayer

Father, I want to thank you for this opportunity to gather together in your name, because you said where there are two or more gathered together in your name, you are right here with us, and we thank you Father in Jesus' name for being right here with us. I ask you, Father, to anoint and appoint us to do your service this day; even though, Father, we may look into the natural realm and see empty seats; but in the spirit realm, you have already chosen those to hear this message and this message will set them totally free. Father, we thank you that you are actually helping our faith, increasing our faith, our trust in you in not going by what we see, but going by what we don't see, Father. I want to thank you for your heavenly host, who's always around us, protecting us. I thank you for those, Father, whom you have led to hear this message and the enemy has put stumbling blocks, obstacles in their way, and I speak against those obstacles and stumbling blocks, and I send the FIRE Power of the Holy Ghost to consume every obstacle and stumbling block that hinders God's child from hearing his Word and being ministered to, as the Lord has chosen and already ordained for them. Father, I thank you. I just thank you, Father, for increasing our trust and faith in you. I thank you Father for the things that you have done or have in store for us to do; the things that we see that you're doing and the things that we cannot see that you're doing for us, Father.

I just thank you for your power, for your Holy Spirit, for your anointing, Father. I ask you to anoint your humble servants, Father, to do your will, your desire this day, Father, in Jesus' mighty name. Father, I just want to say thank you. I thank you, Father, for all of those who have received this message, Father. They are faithful, Father, hoping to and expecting to hear a word from you, Father. Only one word from you, Father, gives us great hope and encouragement that will last the remainder of our days. I just thank you for giving them that one hope, that one word of hope and encouragement this day as they listen to this message and I praise you and thank you in Jesus' name.

MAINTAINING YOUR DELIVERANCE

Jesus Christ is the same yesterday, today and forever (Hebrews 13:8). Whenever our children are in trouble, because of our love and compassion for them, we run to their rescue. When we help them, it is their responsibility to avoid returning to the same situation. Likewise, when Jesus Christ by his Spirit frees our spirit, soul (mind, will, emotions) and body from the enemy, which is the kingdom of darkness-Satan and his demons-it is our responsibility to remain free. Christ Jesus' desire is to set us free from all bondages of the Evil One. He sets us free; and again, it's up to us to maintain our deliverance or freedom. James 4:7 says, "SUBMIT yourselves therefore to God. RESIST the devil, and he will FLEE from you." Therefore; whenever we think of maintaining our deliverance, we should refer to these three steps, SUBMIT-RESIST-FLEE. Praise the living God!

SUBMIT (to God)

When we receive Jesus Christ in our life as Lord, Savior, Deliverer, Counselor and Comforter; we will be in a position to resist the devil. When we submit to him, we will not do what our old nature wants (Galatians 5:16). Jesus Christ came into this world so that we may have life and have it abundantly. He wants us to live a peaceable life (John 14:27). When we submit to God, we will have peace within and without. For Jesus said, "What I am leaving you is peace. I am giving you my peace. I don't give the way the world gives. Don't let yourselves be upset or frightened (John 14:27)." Remember, there's an enemy who doesn't want us to have or live peaceably. He doesn't want us to submit to God, to be free and prosper in

21

any area of our life. He only wants to kill, steal and destroy (John 10:10). When we submit or come closer to God, he will come closer to us. It's like traveling to a certain destination. As we move closer to our destination, it's closer. You notice the place of destination never moved. We're the one that is moving. This is what it means in James 4:8, "Draw near to God, and he will draw near to you." God sits on his throne and he never move. We're supposed to move and submit to him. Praise the living God! When Christ Jesus is in us, by his Spirit, we will have love for each other (John 13:35). We would want to see others set free as we are free. We're the light of God (Matthew 5:14). Therefore; to maintain our deliverance, we must first submit to God.

RESIST (the Devil)

When we submit to God, we are then in a position to resist the devil. Many are the temptations, tribulations and subtle traps of Satan; but our God has given us power and strength to resist them (John 16:33). He's our stronghold, fortress and shield. He's our Protector. By submitting to God, we're able to resist or withstand the forces of evil. We MUST continue to submit to God in order to resist the devil to maintain our deliverance. The ONLY way we can resist the devil is to submit to God's authority. When the devil comes to tempt us, let him find us still submitting to God. Let him see a sign that says, "No Vacancy" because we are filled by and walking in the Spirit. For when we walk in the Spirit, we will not fulfill the desires of the flesh or the old nature (Galatians 5:16).

The Deliverer, Jesus Christ, warned us about what will happen when we fail to submit to God. We will not be able to resist the devil; and since we're not able to resist the devil, he returns to his house and sees a sign that reads, "Vacancy". He sees the house (mind, will, emotions and body) swept, dusted and vacant because of not walking in the Spirit. He moves back in with seven other demon spirits dirtier, more wicked and powerful than it. It found us not submitted to God in a particular area or weakness. It found us regressing to our same old ways. We are now worse than we were before our deliverance (Matthew 12:43-45).

Have you seen a person and asked, "Why are they worse than before?" It's because, after their deliverance, they failed to submit to God; and by doing so, they were not able to resist the devil and devils return. Remember, the enemy is very patient, dear hearts, in what it does. The person may ask, "Why do I have a desire to do this when I never had that desire before." It's because of their failure to maintain their deliverance by submitting to

God's Word. Therefore; they were not able to resist the Devil, and by not being able to resist the devil, he sure didn't flee from them.

FLEE (the Devil)

Galatians 5:19-21 says, "And it is perfectly evident what the old nature does. It expresses itself in sexual immorality, impurity and indecency; involvement with the occult and with drugs; in feuding, fighting, becoming jealous and getting angry; in selfish ambition, factionalism, intrigue and envy; in drunkenness, orgies and things like these. I warn you now as I have warned you before: those who do such things will have no share in the Kingdom of God!" Dear Hearts, when we do such things, devils will not flee or run from us. Instead, we will run in terror from them. Disobedience opens the door to devils, while obedience closes the door. Dear Hearts, we should strip off falsehood. We should speak truth with one another. We should not be angry and sin. In other words, we should not give any space or room to the devil (Ephesians 25-28).

Jesus Christ wants us to maintain our deliverance by continuing in submission to him. Then we'll be able to resist the devil; and in so doing, the devil will flee or run from us. Instead, many of God's dear children are running in terror from the devil. Dear Hearts, this should not be! Jesus Christ has delegated his authority to us to use against Satan and his demons. Luke 10:19 says, "Behold, I give unto you power to tread on serpents and scorpions, and over all the power of the enemy; and nothing shall by any means hurt you." But, when we walk in disobedience to the Lord, this give devils power (or space) to reign and rule in our lives. Therefore; they will not flee or run from us, but we'll run in terror from them.

Yesterday, Today and Forever

Luke 11:14-20 says, "He was expelling a demon that was mute. When the demon had gone out, the man who had been mute spoke; and the people were astounded. But some of them said, "It is by Beelzebub-the ruler of the demons-"that he expels the demons." And others, trying to trap him, demanded from him a sign from Heaven. But he, knowing what they were thinking, said to them, "Every kingdom divided against itself will be ruined, with one house collapsing on another. So if the Adversary too is divided against himself, how can his kingdom survive? I'm asking because you claim it is by Beelzebub that I drive out the demons. If I drive out demons by Beelzebub, by whom do your people drive them out? So, they will be your judges! But if I drive out demons by the **finger of God**, then the Kingdom of God has come upon you!" Jesus is the same yesterday, today and forever (Hebrews 13:8). If he was willing to deliver a person from demons yesterday, he's still willing to do it today. Dear Hearts, Jesus is still doing the same, but it's by his Spirit through his anointed and appointed servants. The 11th Chapter of Luke shows us the compassion of Jesus, the Christ. He loves and cares for us. He wants ALL of us-spirit, soul and body. He doesn't want any of us to be held in captivity by the enemy. He doesn't just want our spirit. He also wants our soul (mind, will, emotions) and body submitted to him. He wants the whole person. He wants us to be totally set free!

Testimony

Jesus once said to me, "Terry, I have some of you, but I don't have ALL of you." I was shocked that the LORD said those words. I thought he had all of me. I worshiped him with my whole heart. I meditated day and night on his Word. Even though I did all these things, I had no idea that demons were living in my mind, will, emotions and body. The Lord knew it, but I didn't and he refused to leave me that way. PRAISE THE LORD! He didn't want anything to come between us and the darkness that was in me came between us. It tried to hinder me in hearing the Lord's voice. Because of God's loving grace and mercy; one day, he sent me to my human helper. He sent me to someone who knew and used their Godly authority. So unknowing to me, he had already commanded the person to lay their hand on me and command those devils to come out. When they did so, I felt something leave my mouth. I later found out from the Lord it was a devil. It came into me due to me not submitting to God. Therefore, I could not resist the devil and he did not flee from me. Instead it entered me. I'm so thankful to God (and to the human vessel) for setting me totally free, so I can serve him in spirit and truth. Dear Hearts, Jesus wanted ALL of me and ALL of you. Praise the living God!

In Conclusion

Dear Hearts, we are in a war and there is no neutral ground. Remember, this is a spiritual warfare. A spiritual battle. The Holy Spirit has kicked the enemy out of our spirit, out of our mind, out of our will, out of our emotions and out of our body. If we're not on God's side, we're his enemy. If we're not helping, we're making things worse (Matthew 12:30). We should ALWAYS remember when a corrupting spirit is expelled or cast out from someone, it goes into the oasis and drifts along looking for an unsuspecting soul who is careless and has not submitted their life to the Lord. When it doesn't find anyone, it says, "I'll go back to my old haunt or where I came from." And then, on return, when it comes back, it find the house swept, dusted and clean. In other words, it finds the person walking in disobedience to God. It then rounds up seven other spirits dirtier than itself and they all moves in, whooping it up. The person is now worse than they were before. Dear Hearts, it is up to us to maintain our deliverance once the Holy Spirit frees us from demons in our spirit, soul (mind, will, emotions) and body.

Jesus Christ delivers and saves! That's who he is-our Deliverer and Savior. He fulfills his promises. Now, we must fulfill our promise in maintaining our deliverance until he returns. For whoever holds out till the end will be delivered (Matthew 24:13). Dear Hearts, we will be COMPLETELY delivered when this mortal body puts on immortality (1 Corinthians 15:52-54). We will then look EXACTLY like Jesus Christ on the inside and the outside. Our body will no longer be made of flesh and blood. Death will be swallowed up in VICTORY!

In the meantime, dear hearts, we MUST walk and live by faith in the Son of God. It is only faith that pleases God. Whatever the LORD does for us, we MUST receive it by faith. Remember, anything not based on faith (or trust) is sin. Let's not be a people that walks by our five senses. A people that only believes what we see, touch or hear. Let's trust God's Word. For he's truth and it's impossible for him to lie. He cannot lie. Let's choose to believe him-his Word. Stay submitted to God and be obedient to him. When the devil comes, remind him of God's Word as Jesus did in the wilderness. Jesus set a PERFECT example for us to follow. Every time the devil came to him, Jesus submitted himself to God and resisted the devil by reminding him of God's Word. Jesus always said, "It is written." After three tries, the devil ran away in terror. Even after the temptations, the devil came back; and each time, he found Jesus submitted to God.

Our Heavenly Father, through Jesus Christ, sent the Holy Spirit as our Counselor and Comforter (John 14:26). He testifies of Jesus Christ. He leads us to all truth and Jesus Christ is truth. We have the same Spirit as Jesus when he was upon this earth. He helps us in our weaknesses or infirmities. He never leaves or forsakes us. He's ALWAYS in us and with us even to the end. Satan and his devils fear him because he is God on earth. The Word of God says when a strong man who is fully equipped for battle guards his own house, his possessions are secure. But when someone stronger attacks and defeats him, he carries off all the armor and weaponry on which the man was depending, and divides up the spoils (Luke 11:21-22). The Holy Spirit is that Strong Man. He is in us if we have received Jesus Christ into our life. Greater is the Holy Spirit in us than devils in the world. Dear Hearts, when you think about maintaining your deliverance, please remember these three steps found in James 4:7, "SUBMIT-RESIST-FLEE". Praise the living God!

Prayer

Oh Lord, you are worthy of all of me. Let your will be done and thy kingdom come over every area of my life and those around me. Let me not be put to shame. Free me from any ancestral bonds. Remove all curses from me, my family and my friends. Give me peace. Break the curse of loneliness and barrenness. Revert all things stolen from me. Give me access to your kingdom. Give me new working parts. Open my spiritual eyes to see. Grant me the desires of my heart. Find me love and pour out an abundance of your Spirit upon me this day. Give me all spiritual blessings due to me. Give me all physical blessings due to me. Forgive me of my sins of arrogance. Allow me to walk with you daily. To hear your voice clearly. To dream dreams. Put your words in my mouth this day forth. Give me all that is due to me from your kingdom. Allow me to see your face. I humble myself before you. Let thy will be done in Jesus' name.

(Prayer inspired by Holy Spirit through Dusti.)

SET YOUR AFFECTION

Focus On Things Above

When we pray, we should always ask the Holy Spirit to pray through us.
He is God on this earth. We truly don't know the root cause of a person's
problem, but the Holy Spirit does. He uses our mouth to make intercession
through us (Romans 8:26-27). One day as I was praying for a person, these
words came out of my mouth, "Set your affection on things above, not on
things on earth." I knew these words were in Scripture; but at that
particular time, I was not thinking about that verse. I then
IMMEDIATELY knew the Lord by his Spirit was praying through me for
this individual and the Holy Spirit was making known the person's root
cause for their problems. I then decided to dissect that verse. I began by
looking at its meaning in the dictionary and found that the word "set"
means "to initiate action or process"; and "affection" means "love,
fondness, warmth, friendliness and tenderness"; and "things" means
"affairs, which is general matter or circumstances".

Dear Hearts, when we don't initiate action in giving our love on the affairs
(or circumstances) that comes from above, we create a spirit of loneliness,
doubt and negativity which comes from this earth because Satan exists and
operates on the earth. We should initiate action in the things we love and
are fond of that comes from above and not expect those things to come
from the earth. In other words, we should focus our affection, our love,
fondness and warmth on the things which comes from God (Colossians
3:2). Matthew 6:33 says, "But seek first the Kingdom and his righteousness,
and all these things will be given to you as well." What is righteousness? It
is being in right standing with God. We can only receive right standing

with God, the Father, through Jesus Christ. Accepting what Jesus Christ did on the cross for us. The Lord wants us to set our affection or focus on him and not on the things of the earth. The things on earth are temporary. He is Everlasting Life. Praise the living God!

When we speak truth, the devil doesn't like it! Since he's a spirit and does not have a body with a mouth to speak, he will use a human vessel to express his thoughts and feelings. So when he finds someone who has yielded the members of their body to him, he will speak and act through them. Dear Hearts, we're to continue to set our affection on things above by allowing the Holy Spirit to speak and act through us in Jesus' mighty name. Praise the living God! Therefore, whenever we minister the Word of God or make up our mind to focus on the things of God and set our affection on things above and begin to do it through conversation and deed, the enemy will find a yielded vessel to tell us, "I don't like what you're doing!" They will even scoff and mock you. If you're a female servant of God, the devil will even say, "You don't have any business preaching the gospel." Dear Hearts, in spite of the devil's threats, we have to continue to set our affection on things above. We cannot focus on what the devil says through others because they're focused on things on this earth. What we need to do is continue keeping our focus like the Apostle Paul (Romans 8:38-39) on Jesus Christ, his righteousness and Kingdom which are the things above and we will experience joy and peace in our life.

Where Is Our Affection?

Most people, young and old, are having problems in their relationships. They're focusing their attention on the man (or woman) on this earth. They don't have peace, joy and happiness. As long as the man (or woman) acts the way they desire, they're happy. The moment they do not, they're sad. We must remember that a person who is not focusing their affection on the things above are wishy-washy. The Lord says they're "double minded and unstable in all their ways (James 1:8)." One day they may be nice to you; and the next day, they'll be ugly to you and cause you to be confused. Why? Because you set your affection on the things on this earth. The things that you love and are fond of. You continued to focus on the things on earth instead of thinking and focusing on the things above which is Christ Jesus, the Kingdom of God and His righteousness; for Jesus gives us peace-not as the world gives (John 14:27)

When we set our affection on things of this earth, it creates problems in our life. We're to love our family, but we're not to set our affection or thoughts on our family. We should love our family indirectly through Christ Jesus. We're not to worry about our children. When we do, it causes us to become sick because we've set our affection directly on them. We're told not to do that and to set our affection on things above, on Jesus Christ, the Kingdom of God and his righteousness. When we obey God as he said, he will work on our behalf on earth in our circumstances. He'll start working in our child's heart. Sometimes we try to do the work of the Holy Spirit and we cannot do it. It is his responsibility to convict a person of sin, righteousness and judgement (John 16:8). As parents, we should remember when our children are adults and are wayward, it's not our responsibility to convict them of their wrongdoings or sins. It's the Holy Spirit's responsibility. The Lord wants us to set our affection on him and then he will work on our behalf through his Spirit in convicting our children of sin, righteousness and judgement.

He wants us to do the same regarding our spouse. Our spouse may be misbehaving and it worries us to the point we may say, "You know what? I can't take this no longer! Here's my bill of divorcement." Do you see what happens when we set our affection on things on the earth instead of setting it on things above which is in Christ Jesus? Dear Hearts, even in that situation, when we set our affection on things above which is in Christ Jesus, he will fight our battle for us. As we worship and pray for our spouse and KEEP asking according to Luke 11:9-10, the Holy Spirit will work on our behalf and will convict our spouse of sin, righteousness and judgement. We don't have to give our spouse a bill of divorcement. We just need to set our affection on things above and not on circumstances on earth. Mankind says, "If you don't get along with your spouse, just do away with him or her and get another one." That is not God's perfect will. As children of God, he wants us to set our affection on the things above. When we set our affection on things above which is in Christ Jesus in seeking his kingdom and righteousness, regardless of the circumstances that surrounds us on earth, we will be full of joy and peace within and no devil in hell or on this earth or in the heavenlies can take that away from us. That's why it's very important that we set our affection on the things above and not on the things on this earth.

Words Reflect the Heart

Whenever we have problems in life and they overwhelm us, we need to ask ourselves this question, "Where am I setting my affection? Is it on the things of this earth which are the general matters or circumstances of this earth or am I setting my affection on the things above, the general matters and circumstances that are above?" We also need to watch the words that come out of our mouths such as, "You're getting on my nerves!" When we say such words, we're setting our affection on things on this earth and not on the things above. We shouldn't say such to anyone and especially our spouse or children. It is not love coming from above. It is hate and anger coming from below. We really need to be careful and watch even the words that come out of our mouth because the words that come out of the mouth can either cause a person to set their affection on things above or things on this earth. It's important to judge EVERY word that comes out of our mouth. Have you ever noticed what comes out of our mouth will either lead a person to set their affection on things above or on the earth? What comes out of the mouth comes from the heart. For the Word of God says, "Out of abundance of a man's heart he speaks (Luke 6:43-45)." Whatever is in your heart is what you're going to speak. If the words of our mouth are causing people to set their affection (love, fondness, warmth, friendliness and tenderness) on the things of this earth and not the things above, then we need to ask the Holy Spirit to come into our heart and do his inward work that only he can do.

It Begins at Home

Many homes are in a condition of extreme confusion, agitation and commotion. They may appear to be peaceful outwardly; but inwardly, everything is torn to pieces. There's no peace, rest and joy. Spouses are at war with one another. What does that mean? It means the head of the home is not setting their affection on the things above. As the LORD once said to me, "No head! It's dead!" Meaning when the head is cut off, the body dies. Whenever the husband (the head of the home) is not in his proper place, which is in the presence of God, the family suffers. When Adam left the Presence of God, his family (at that time, it was only his wife and later, his children) suffered. When we fail to set our affection on the things above, dear hearts, we will suffer. In most homes, television is one of the greatest hindrances. Sometimes, we need to just turn it off. What we allow to show on our television will show us where we're setting our affection. Is it on the things above or the things of this earth? After turning the television off, bring your family together and pray and teach them about seeking the Kingdom of God and his righteousness. The Holy Spirit will saturate your home; and when strangers come into your house, they will feel God's presence. There will be people who are full of devils and when they get to your door, they're going to say, "I cannot go in there!" Why? Because the presence of God is so strong and they cannot go in because they have set their affection on the things of the earth.

Dear Hearts, the Lord is telling us to set our affection on the things above not on the things on earth. He wants us to focus our mind on him. When we focus on something, we set it as a target and we don't go off course, because we have a specific aim. That's what the Lord wants us to do. He wants us to aim our mind on the Kingdom of God and his righteousness and He will give us the things we need. Jesus walked on this earth for 33½ years. He set his affection on the things of God, on the things above and what did the Father do? The Father provided and added everything he needed in order to live on the earth; and he shall provide all our needs (Philippians 4:19).

No Earthly Good? To Who?

It's important that we don't repeat the saying, "You're so heavenly minded, you're no earthly good." Such saying is from the enemy to convince us to focus on the things of this earth and not on the things from above. According to God's Word, we are to be heavenly minded. There's no such thing as being so heavenly minded that we're no earthly good. When we are heavenly minded, of course, we're no earthly good to the devil! Therefore, whenever we choose to say such words, are we also saying it to Jesus? Look how heavenly minded Jesus was when he walked on this earth and he sure was earthly good. Dear Hearts, the saying did not originate from the word of God. It's contrary to the Word of God. It should not be in the mouth of God's children. When such words are spoken, it is Jesus who Satan is actually referring to because he was the First Person to be so heavenly minded that he was no earthly good to Satan. Dear Hearts, just as Jesus Christ, we're to be so heavenly minded that we're no earthly good to Satan and his demons. The Lord wants us to be heavenly minded. When he tells us to set our affection on things above and not on things of earth, he's telling us to be heavenly minded. When we are heavenly minded, we will be some earthly good to God. When we set our affection on things above, then we are heavenly minded and some earthly good to the Lord. But when we set our affection on things of the earth, then we are no earthly good to the Lord. Therefore, here's proof that the saying "You're so heavenly minded, you're no earthly good" did not come from God. It's a deception and trap of the enemy to keep us always focusing on the things of the earth. Selah (think about it).

Testimony

When I was a teenager, my mother would force me to attend church service with her. I didn't want to go, but she forced me anyway. Today, I'm thankful to God she did that; but at that time, I was not. I was my mother's only child. My grandmother had children along with her children and I had uncles and aunts around the same age. I noticed the aunt whom I was only a year older. When my grandmother forced her to attend church, she would embarrass my grandmother in church services. She did this every time my grandmother forced her to attend church. It worked so I decided to do the same to my mother. Hoping that my mother would stop forcing me to attend church service with her. In the next service, I kept an angry look on my face in hopes that it would embarrass my mother and she would stop forcing me to attend church with her. To my amazement, my mother didn't pay any attention at all to me and acted as if I was not even there. She was not concerned about what I was doing to embarrass her and did not care what people thought about it. She kept her focus on things above and not on the earth. Today, I'm happy that she did not have her affection directly on me. Her affection was on the Kingdom of God and his righteousness and being in right standing with God.

Years later, I finally chose to set my affection on things above. When I received the Lord into my life, I asked him to give me a change of heart because I knew I was full of darkness. I asked him to show me my heart and he did. I saw myself going down into the darkness of a pit. The further I went, the darker it became. Until finally, I no longer could bare it and screamed, "No more and the Lord brought me up." I then said, "God! My heart is evil and wicked!" At that time, I was a teenager. Many people would have thought, "You're a teenager, you never did much sin." Dear Hearts, ALL unrighteous is sin. There's no such thing as a little sin or a big sin because all unrighteousness is sin. Remember, not even a speck of sin is going to enter into God's kingdom. It's like having a beautiful white wedding dress and there's a tiny spot on it. Would you look at the remaining of the dress and ignore the spot? Of course not! That spot would look so huge on your white wedding garment and you'll throw it away to get a spotless one. Likewise, all unrighteousness is sin in the eyes of God. I thank him that he changed my heart and continues changing me. He's giving me his heart, compassion, love and affection. That's what happens when we focus our affection on things above. Shalom.

FIRE PRAYERS AGAINST SPIRIT SPOUSES (AND FRIENDS)

What are Spirit Spouses?

Most people are unaware there are demonic spirit spouses-spirit husband and spirit wife. We know and understand about human spouses, but not spirit spouses. Our Heavenly Father created marriage for the human race which is honorable and the bed not defiled (Hebrews 13:4). Jesus says in his Word there is no marriage (Matthew 22:30) or gender (Galatians 3:28) in the spirit realm.

Satan does contrary to the will of God. Since God was the One who created and ordained marriage between a human male and female, Satan twisted this truth. He used for his glory the same concept, but for evil. He assigns spirit spouses to human beings in order to kill, steal and destroy their destinies in Christ Jesus. His aim is only to kill, steal and destroy (John 10:10).

What are FIRE Prayers?

FIRE prayers were revealed to Evangelist King by the Holy Spirit as she conducted deliverance sessions via the phone line or at the Holy Ghost FIRE Deliverance Meeting of *The Children's Mite*. According to James 5:16, they are proven to be effective and fervent in the spirit realm in setting captives free from spirit husband, spirit wife and EVERY spirit not of the Holy Spirit. If you have not done so already, follow us at www.vimeo.com/thechildrensmite for more Holy Ghost FIRE Prayers. As the Holy Spirit leads and reveals, more prayer points will be added in Jesus' name.

Survey Questions

The survey is designed to reveal the existence of spirit husband and spirit wife, aka spirit spouses. Christ Jesus died for our FREEDOM (Galatians 5:1). He wants us to be totally free in our mind, free in our will, free in our emotions and free in our body to worship our Heavenly Father in spirit and truth (John 4:23-24). If you answer 'Yes' to any of the questions below, a spirit spouse is actively working in and against your life and hindering your destiny in Christ Jesus.

Do I Have a Spirit Spouse?

1.   Have you ever been molested? Molestation is not just restricted to penetration, but also include fondling by a child or an adult. It can be as simple as playing Mom and Dad games as a child or hearing someone talking in a sexual manner in childhood. I often stress to the person the importance of asking the Holy Spirit to bring back to remembrance that which the LORD wants to be remembered because devils will block the person's memory in order to prevent exposure of the 'root' to their problem.

2.   Have you ever been raped? A person can be raped by human beings, demon spirits and/or human spirits.

3.   Do you have sexual lust?

4.   Do you have sex in your dreams? Some people have sex in their dreams and are enjoying it. Dear Hearts that is not the Lord. If you have sex in your dreams and the person has the appearance of your spouse, it's not your spouse. It's a spirit spouse. It's not your human spouse. Or if it's a boyfriend or girlfriend, somebody you know. If you are even having sex in your dreams, period, dear heart, that is a demon spirit-a spirit spouse.

5.   Does it seem like you're being "forced" to remain unmarried-every relationship ends up in disappointment? You've been engaged several times and each time for some reason, you have a change of mind. It's like you've been forced to stay unmarried. That's the sign of a spirit spouse.

6.   Do you masturbate?

7.   Do you watch pornography?

8.   Is there idolatry in your family lineage?

9.   Is there witchcraft in your family lineage?

These questions are evidences or signs of a spirit spouse; and only Jesus Christ with his chosen servant can set you totally free from that ungodly covenant of idolatry. Dear hearts, I've learned that it's good to allow the Holy Spirit to reveal the root cause of how spirit spouse entered into our mind, will, emotions and/or body. Knowing this truth, will help us to keep doors closed; and not only that, we are able to help others become free. Again, as you say the prayers out loud and experience any uneasiness or agitation, immediately contact us. You will need someone to join their faith with your faith for your complete deliverance in casting out the strong man (Mark 3:27). Praise the living God!

FIRE Prayers

Suppose a human thief or stranger was trying to break into your house? You wouldn't command them to leave your house quietly. You would shout out loud, "Get Out!" Likewise, the FIRE prayers need to be spoken out loud and aggressively. From your heart, say the FIRE prayers out loud:

1.   Father, in the name of Jesus, YOU SAID when two or more are gathered in your Son's name, you are with us (Matthew 18:20).

2.   Father, in the name of Jesus, YOU SAID whatsoever I bind or loose on earth; You will bind or loose in heaven (Matthew 18:18).

3.   Right NOW, in the name of Jesus, SPIRIT SPOUSE, I COMMAND YOU to COME OUT of my mind, COME OUT of my will, COME OUT of my emotions and COME OUT of my body!

4.   I bind, in the name of Jesus, EVERY spirit that is not of the Holy Spirit and cast you at my Heavenly Father to deal with as He wills.

5.   Spirit spouse, PACK YOUR LOAD AND GO, in Jesus' name!

6. By faith, I take the SCISSORS of God and cut and sever the spiritual umbilical cord of ungodly covenant and contract of witchcraft and idolatry!

7. I command spiritual poison to COME OUT of my stomach and body in Jesus' name!

8. Spirit snake, COME OUT!

9. Spirit Jezebel, COME OUT!

10. EVERY spirit not of the Holy Ghost, COME OUT!

11. By faith, I take the BLOOD OF JESUS and pour over EVERY known and unknown covenant and contract in the name of Jesus. Disconnect in Jesus' name!

12. Father, send your angels in the spirit realm and grab EVERY spirit that is not of You and send them where You desire to send them in Jesus' name.

13. HOLY GHOST FIRE, BURN! Burn everything that is not of You.

14. HOLY GHOST FIRE! HOLY GHOST FIRE! BURN! BURN! BURN!

15. Holy Ghost give me a CLEAN SWEEP!

16. Give me a CLEAN FLUSH by Your MIGHTY FIRE in Jesus' name!

17. RANSACK OR SEARCH my mind!

18. RANSACK OR SEARCH my will!

19. RANSACK OR SEARCH my emotions!

20. RANSACK OR SEARCH my body! In Jesus' name.

21. Give me a CLEAN Flushing!

22. Give me a CLEAN Sweep!

23. Holy Spirit, leave no compartment or area untouched by your MIGHTY FIRE!

24. FIRE! FIRE! FIRE! BURN! BURN! BURN!

25. BURN from the crown of my head to the sole of my feet!

26. BURN! BURN! BURN!

27. FIRE Power of the Holy Ghost, set ABLAZE EVERYTHING not of you in Jesus' name!

28. Set ABLAZE! Set ABLAZE! Set ABLAZE!

29. FIRE! FIRE! FIRE!

30. THANK YOU, Father. My mind is NOW FREE to serve You. My will is NOW FREE to serve You! My emotions are NOW FREE to serve You. My body is NOW FREE to serve You. Father, fill me to overflow with your precious Spirit. Fill EVERY void and empty space in me by your mighty power of the Holy Ghost. Father, I thank you! I'm FREE!

Contact Us

Dear Hearts, if you experienced any uneasiness, agitation; and/or you just don't want to say the prayers, you need to submit the Deliverance Request Submission Form located on our website. There's a strong man in you that needs to come out and you need someone to join their faith with your faith. Someone who will believe God's Word for your total deliverance. Someone who God has appointed and anointed in coming against and throwing out the strong man. That's if you experience any uneasiness or agitation or if you didn't want to say the prayers. Again, there is a strong man in you that need to come out of God's house (the mind, will, emotions and body). Remember, the soul (mind, will and emotions) that sins is the one that will die (Ezekiel 18:20).

Words of Encouragement

IF you received the FIRE Prayers by and in faith, dear heart, you are now free. You are free from any internal interruptions and preventions that hindered your progress in life. You are free from devils living in your mind, will, emotions and body-forcing you to sin against God. You are free! Now, walk by faith and live by faith in the Son of God. Stay free! Submit your life to the Lord in all your ways. Be obedient unto his commands. Make sure you join a local church where the pastor is leading you back to your Lord and Savior, Jesus Christ. Walk in your new found freedom in Christ Jesus. Worship and magnify him! Thank him because he did not have to do it, but he did. Thank him for freeing you. Thank him for his mercy and grace. Thank him. He's there with you now. Praise his holy name. Say, thank you Jesus, thank you, and always receive of him by faith in Jesus' name.

Christ Jesus sets us free, but we MUST maintain our deliverance. Remember, the Deliverer said, "When an unclean spirit comes out of a person, it travels through dry country seeking rest and does not find it. Then it says to itself, 'I will return to the house I left.' When it arrives, it finds the house standing empty, swept clean and put in order. Then it goes and takes with it seven other spirits more evil than itself, and they come and live there-so that in the end, the person is worse off than he was before."

Dear Hearts, remembering these steps in James 4:7, SUBMIT-RESIST-FLEE, will help us to maintain our deliverance. Stay submitted in Jesus' name. Shalom.

Prayer

Heavenly Father, thank you for anointing and appointing this message for your dear children to be free from strangers within their mind, will, emotions and body. Thank you Father, there's nothing impossible with you; for the Holy Spirit's mighty FIRE, ransacks, searches, rumbles and destroys EVERYTHING not of him in Jesus' mighty name. Thank you for purifying your dear children and cleaning them with the Blood of your Son, Christ Jesus. Amen.

Testimonies

Good day. How are you and your family? I hope fine. I would like to share my testimony on how God delivered me from a spirit husband. Last night, I was listening to the podcast on, "Fire Prayers against spirit spouses and friends", and as you prayed these prayers, though I did not manifest, I felt the peace of the Lord flood my soul, and I received by faith that I had been delivered of these wicked spirits. I just want to firstly say, Thank you Heavenly Father for my deliverance, in Jesus' Name" and I also want to say thank you Evangelist King for letting God use you to set the captives free. I ask God to bless you and your household abundantly, in the Mighty Name of Jesus Christ, Amen.—Annette (USA)

I would like to say thank you thank you thank you. It is through your audio prayer for spirit spouses, and our heavenly father and Jesus that I have felt peace. While listening to it, I felt a tug at my heart and my mind was filled with the vision of shadows slipping away from me. I knew these were attached to me somehow. Afterwards, I felt stronger and more at peace with myself. I know something miraculous and wonderful happened when I listened to you that day, and is still happening. Thank you. Praise the Lord and may he continue his great work through you.—Mel (UK)

I went through the fire prayers for deliverance from a spirit spouse. I just wanted to have someone join their faith with me and any other deliverance necessary. Thank you all so much, in advance.—Nikki (USA)

Evangelist King, I heard about you from my daughter and I downloaded the Fire Prayers. My daughter prayed over me and I couldn't sleep last night so I'm requesting that you pray over me again to ensure deliverance from this "Spirit Husband". I want deliverance so that I can be a living witness to God and others that "whom the Son sets free is free indeed. Thank you for your attention to my request and may God bless you and your husband for the awesome work you all are doing for God's Kingdom.—Barbara (USA)

Kindly find attached the translation in Armenian of "Do I Have a Spirit Spouse?" prayer. I thank Lord Jesus from my heart for the deliverance he gave me by your prayers and I thank you also for your care and help. May Jesus bless you more and more, dear Terry. While translating it, I had to read it over and over and yawned all the time till tears flew down my eyes and I was filled with peace and joy.—Arshag (Lebanon)

I just said the prayers. I've had dark shapes follow me wherever I've lived. I don't know if I feel agitated after saying the prayer, but my nerves are trembling a bit.—Anne (USA)

As I says these prayers, I began to burp and my fingers begin to feel numb, uneasy in my chest. I also notice that I had to force myself to listen and continue the prayers.—Althea (UK)

I have heard some deliverance prayers online during the last days and therefore believe that I need deliverance.—Monja (Armenia)

Dear Hearts, I would love to hear your testimony. Go to our website and submit your testimony. I would love to hear your story, hear what God has done. Some of you, as the FIRE prayers were spoken, there were manifestations as demons were leaving. I want you to share that. Those of you who didn't and you felt the peace of God, you have to remember it is still God. God is the one who chooses whether he is going to allow demons to make themselves known or not. Many of you were set free and the demons left quietly. They came into you quietly, they left quietly and you felt the presence of the peace of God. I want to hear your testimony.

It encourages me when I read your testimony; because you need to realize that this message is by faith. I cannot see you and it's good to read testimonies. It's by faith that I know God's done what he said he would do. I want to hear your testimony. Remember, we overcome the devil, not only by the Blood of the Lamb, but also by the word of our testimony. We share our testimony, one with another, about the great things Jesus has done for us. We encourage each other in the Faith. It also encourage others in letting them see that the same God who set you free will set them free. So dear hearts, let us know your testimony and how helpful this message of deliverance was to you. Again, thank you and praise his holy name. Shalom.

FIRE PRAYER FOR PREGNANCY

Don't Delay Obedience

I received a message from one of my international friends. For several weeks, the Lord had been beckoning her to contact me to be delivered from spirit spouse-spirit husband. As instructed, I never received the required Deliverance Request Submission Form located on our website. When I asked about it, she said, "I tried, but having problems." The Holy Spirit then told me that the spirit husband prevented her from submitting it. It knew when she got in contact with me, she would be delivered from it. A few months later, I received another message from her. She said, "Evangelist King, I lost my baby." Immediately I knew that spirit husband was the one who terminated her pregnancy. Jesus Christ warned her by sending her for deliverance. He wanted to set her totally free and she was slow in responding.

Dear Hearts, the moment we hear God's voice, we should not harden our hearts (Hebrews 3:15). Don't be slow to respond to God. Don't delay obedience. Quickly do as the Lord instructs. Satan's aim is only to kill, steal and destroy (John 10:10). Jesus had nothing to do with the loss of her child. It was spirit husband (and friends). After reading her message, I became spiritually angry and decided to do a message and prayer especially for women who are pregnant and married women (and men) who desire to birth children and cannot.

All Have Sinned

Whenever a married couple has problems in birthing children; most likely a spirit spouse is involved. Due to unfaithfulness in keeping our bodies pure, holy and righteous; spirit spouses are assigned to the human being in order to kill, steal and destroy their destiny in Christ Jesus and their marriage. The Lord instructs us to, "Run from sexual immorality! Every other sin a person commits is outside the body, but the fornicator sins against his own body (1 Corinthians 6:18).

We all have sinned and come short of earning God's praise (Romans 3:23). This is true; but because of Christ Jesus' grace and mercy, we are forgiven and free. Free to do what? We are free to choose to do what is right or wrong (Deuteronomy 30:15). When we choose to do what is wrong, we can repent and the Lord will forgive us; but he also says, "Sin no more (John 8:11)." When he say to sin no more, that closes the door from the Evil One in hindering our blessings here on earth. Regardless of the blessings (e.g., fruit of the womb, financial, joy, peace, happiness, etc.). Also when we obey God, it keeps the devil hands out of our business. Therefore; the person we should tell to stay out of our business is not human beings, but devils. We should kick them out by submitting ourselves to God in remaining obedient.

Remember, these prayers are for women who are pregnant and/or those who are married and cannot have children. If you're not married and desire to have children while not being married, don't pray these prayers because you're not walking in obedience to God. You're sinning against God because sex outside of marriage is sin. Let's not receive pregnancy lightly. Every time a woman becomes pregnant, she is risking her life. Today there are many options to take in childbirth. In order to escape the pain, women are offered epidurals and C-sections. Some women don't even need C-sections, but they request it anyway. I have noticed in Africa, women are adamant against epidurals and C-sections. While in America, women want to have babies without pain and enjoy while giving birth so they will request epidurals and some will request a C-section. There's nothing wrong with having an epidural or C-section. It's wrong whenever the person doesn't need it and they request it. Their concern is for themselves and not for the baby. I truly believe if more young girls were not given epidurals and only given a C-Section when needed, they would think twice before becoming pregnant again. Selah (think about it).

Remember spirit spouses' aim is to kill, to steal and to destroy. I have observed that some people know that they have a spirit lover (or spirit spouse). They see the evidence and refuse to be delivered from it because they say they're enjoying the sex. Yuck! On the other hand, others do not know. Dear Hearts, if you have tattoos on your body, that's evidence that spirit lover is lurking in you. Who do you think it is that suggested to get them? To defy the Lord thy God who is the creator of our body? It is spirit spouse (and friends). They're suggesting it to you! Whenever you feel movement in your body and you're not pregnant, that is spirit spouse (and friends). Some of you who are pregnant and you feel the baby move; but it seems like there's another peculiar movement and you're not sure it's the baby; that's spirit husband and it opened the door for spirit snake.

Dear Hearts, this is important! When a woman becomes pregnant, the enemy, Satan and his devils, are angry. They hate LIFE and will suggest to abort the pregnancy-to kill the baby. Who do you think is making that suggestion? It's certainly not the woman! It's spirit lover-spirit husband; and sometimes, also spirit wife in the father of the child. Again, they hate LIFE because LIFE comes from God. They hate anything that our Heavenly Father created and love. They hate you and me. Why? Because we were made in our Heavenly Father's image and likeness. In other words, we look just like our Father. Therefore, when devils look on us, they are reminded of our Heavenly Father, their creator. Of course, the evil aspects of them the Father did not create. They are fallen angels.

Dear Hearts, I had to share a little knowledge with you so you can get an understanding of what's going on in your life. Time is short and Jesus is soon to come. I know you have heard that many times; but TRULY, time is short and Jesus is soon to come. Jesus is coming back for a holy temple. Our body is his temple (1 Corinthians 6:19-20). He's not coming back for a temple full of snakes. Even you don't want to go dwell in a place that is full of snakes. As a matter of fact, you wouldn't even want to go to a church house that was full of snakes. Jesus said he's not coming back for a temple full of snakes and I'm referring to spirit snakes.

FIRE Prayers

Listen and receive the FIRE prayer for pregnancy to root out spirit spouses, spirit snakes, spirit Jezebel, spirit death, spirit destruction and EVERY spirit not of the Holy Ghost in Jesus' mighty name! Suppose a human thief or stranger was trying to break into your house? You wouldn't command them to leave your house quietly. You would shout out loud, "Get Out!" Likewise, the FIRE prayers need to be spoken out loud and aggressively. From your heart, say the FIRE prayers out loud:

1. In the name of Jesus; spirit husband and spirit wife, come to attention! For the Blood of Jesus commands you to come to attention right now! In Jesus' name, come out! Come out of God's temple! Come out! Come out of God's house! Come out of the will! Come out of the emotions! Come out of the mind! Come out of the body!

2. Pack your load and GO! Pack everything that belongs to you, spirit lover, spirit husband and wife and GET OUT in Jesus' mighty name!

3. Holy Ghost FIRE! BURN from the crown of the head to the soles of the feet! Flush and sweep out everything that is not of you! Flush out all spiritual poison and darkness! Flush out spiritual umbilical cord in Jesus' mighty name!

4. Holy Ghost FIRE! BURN in the belly, BURN in the womb, BURN in the stomach, BURN in the mouth, BURN in the ears, BURN in the eyes and BURN any where there are openings and holes. BURN in Jesus' mighty name! BURN, FLUSH and SWEEP out everything that is not of you!

5. Spirits of killing, stealing and destruction, loose and let go in Jesus' mighty name!

6. Father, in Jesus' mighty name, I shall be fruitful and multiply as you commanded in Genesis 1:28.

7. Holy Ghost FIRE! Continue to BURN in Jesus' mighty name; for the Blood of Jesus has forgiven us and our ancestors.

8. Holy Ghost FIRE! The Blood of Jesus all over the body! The Blood of Jesus all over tattoos! The Blood of Jesus, BURN!

9. Holy Ghost FIRE! BURN illegal holes and piercings in the body! BURN in Jesus' mighty name. BURN! BURN! BURN!

10. Holy Ghost FIRE! BURN everything in the mind, will, emotions and body that don't move, don't walk, don't talk and don't sound like you in the mighty name of Jesus. BURN!

11. Father, in Jesus' mighty name, send your angels and gather every spirit that is not of you. Send them where you desire to send them in Jesus' name.

12. Holy Ghost FIRE! SEARCH and BURN every illegal being that attached itself to the baby! BURN in Jesus' mighty name! BURN!

13. Spirits of darkness! COME OUT! Loose the baby in Jesus' name! Holy Ghost FIRE! BURN! BURN! BURN!

14. Sickness and disease! BURN in Jesus' mighty name! BURN!

15. Father, I thank you for giving the mother and child a blood transfusion of the Blood of your Son, Jesus Christ. I thank you that mother and child are healthy. The pregnancy is normal and healthy in Jesus' mighty name.

16. I thank you Father for your protection around the mother, the father and the baby in Jesus' name. Thank you for setting your daughter, your son and the child totally free in Jesus' mighty name. Thank you for this pregnancy and for the child who will grow up to be that which you call them to be. Thank you for filling them to overflow with your Spirit. Let your Spirit linger and hoover in and around the child, the mother and the father in the name of Jesus. Father, I thank you in Jesus' mighty name.

17. Thank you Father for cleaning your house (temple) this day. Thank you for cleaning the womb, for removing all manner of evil objects that were placed in the womb to hinder from conceiving. I thank you that you burned all evil tools by the FIRE of the Holy Ghost. I thank you for TOTAL freedom to conceive and to raise children in the nurturing and admonition of the Lord. In Jesus' name, thank you, Father. Amen.

Testimony

Our youngest daughter had our first grandchild seven months ago. I used the same prayers to pray over her and the baby. The enemy tried to attack her and the baby, but the Holy Spirit led me to put my hands on her stomach and pray. This message serves as a point of contact for me to pray with you as well. The doctors told her because of having low blood platelets, she needed a C-Section. We prayed and trusted the Lord in that she would not need it when the time came for delivery. Throughout her pregnancy, her blood platelets continued to be low and even lower; but we kept believing the Lord would see her through and she would not need to have a C-Section. Dear Hearts, when she went into labor, her blood platelets were still low and she still had a normal delivery without a C-Section. I knew the Holy Spirit hovered around my daughter and grandchild. The devil had to take its hands off of my daughter's pregnancy and my grandchild in the womb. Dear hearts, we need to ask the Lord for his protection in all situations in our life; and believe when we ask him because he will do it. Praise the living God!

In Conclusion

Dear Hearts, you are free! Your body is free to conceive! Your child is free! Thank you Jesus! Glory to his holy name! Now, PRAISE HIM! The Lord set you free because that spirit lover that was in you planned to kill you and/or the child, but God did not allow it. Those of you who have already given birth before knowing about the FIRE Prayers and your child was born healthy, it's crucial that you still say the prayers. You may say, "I had a good pregnancy and a healthy pregnancy. My baby is fine. I don't need to say those prayers." Yes! You still need to say the prayers! The reason is because that spirit may have hidden in the womb with your child and when your child was born, it was attached to your child. It's waiting for the opportune time to manifest in and through the child. You don't want that spirit in your child! Your child may look fine on the outside; but on the inside, that spirit is there. Again, it's waiting for an opportune time to manifest and express itself. You don't want that thing in your child. You want that thing completely out.

IF you have already delivered your baby and would like to pray FIRE prayers over your child, then visit our website at www.deliverance.thechildrensmite.org/prayer. The FIRE Prayer in written format is located at the bottom of the page. You can download and print it out. Dear Hearts, speak the prayer over your child because that spirit is hiding deep in darkness in your child's mind, will, emotions and body. I will also advise you to have the prayers prayed over you. Get another child of God who has been delivered and is anointed and appointed by God to pray deliverance prayers over you. Then when you get free, you can pray over your child and your child will be free. Praise the living God! Dear Hearts, don't allow the enemy to harden your heart. Get free so your family can get free. And then stay free by continuing in obedience to God.

Dear Hearts, let's not do as my international friend. Even to this day, spirit husband (and friends) convinced her not to pursue deliverance as the Lord instructed. Don't allow the enemy to harden your heart. The moment you hear God's voice, don't turn away. He warns us for a reason. Be obedient and later you'll see why the Lord instructed you to do so. Shalom.

The Children's Mite † Evangelist King
DELIVERANCE PRAYER

Father, you said where two or three are gathered together in your Son's name, you are in the midst. You said whatever we bind and loose on earth, you will bind and loose in the heavens. Father, we also know there is no such thing as distance in the spirit realm. Father, I thank you right now for the one coming in agreement for their healing and deliverance in Jesus' name. Father, I thank you that right now through this book you are cleaning and rearranging your house in the mind, will, emotions and body and driving out EVERY spirit that doesn't move, walk, talk, act or sound like you. Father, in Jesus' name, I thank you for the mighty FIRE POWER of the Holy Ghost.

Right now, in the name of Jesus, I take my authority and command spirit lover, spirit husband, spirit wife and EVERY spirit not of the Holy Ghost to come to attention! You pack your load and get out! Get out of their mind! Get out of their will! Get out of their emotions! Get out of their body! In Jesus' name! Holy Ghost FIRE all over their body! Holy Ghost FIRE in their mind, in their will, in their emotions! Holy Ghost FIRE burn everything that is not of you. Clean and sweep the house by your mighty FIRE! FIRE of the Holy Ghost! BURN in Jesus' name! Loose and leave God's property, you spirits of killing, stealing and destruction, in the name of Jesus!

The Blood of Jesus separates, detaches and disconnects everything that Satan has connected in their mind, in their will, in their emotions and in their body. Holy Ghost FIRE continue to consume everything that is not of you! Clean the house in Jesus' mighty name! Disconnect everything not of you! Separate and detach them from every known and unknown

48

covenant of idolatry and witchcraft by the Blood of Jesus. Come out! Holy Ghost FIRE continue to burn and sweep the house clean. Leave no area or compartment untouched by your mighty FIRE. Holy Ghost FIRE continue to burn everything that's not of you out of the mind! Come out and pack your load and GO in Jesus' name! Never to return, physically or spiritually, in the name of Jesus!

Father, fill them to overflow with your Spirit. Let them feel your love, warmth and compassion in Jesus' name. Fill their mind. Fill their will. Fill their emotions. Fill their body. In Jesus' name. Father, I thank you for the angels you have dispatched right now to gather EVERY spirit that doesn't walk, talk or sound like you, and dealing with them and putting them where you desire. Father, I thank you for your fiery protection of the Holy Ghost. Father, thank you for filling them with your FIRE and protecting all their properties. Father, give them peace in their heart, mind, will, emotions and body in Jesus' mighty name. Thank you, Father, in Jesus' name. Amen.

ABOUT THE AUTHOR

Mrs. Terry B. King aka Evangelist King continues to answer the supernatural call of and by God, to do the work of an evangelist through *The Children's Mite*, a ministry of salvation, healing, deliverance and giving, with outreach ministry that includes deliverance and feeding programs, as well as healing and deliverance services. She is Founder and CEO. Gifted with a compassion for the lost and neglected, she strives to share the "Good News" of Christ Jesus with everyone she meets. Understanding the Word of the LORD God through His anointed servants, "The work I'm doing in you, no man will be able to get the glory," she continues to strive to share the "Good News" of her Risen LORD Jesus to a physical and spiritual impoverished world †

www.ingramcontent.com/pod-product-compliance
Lightning Source LLC
Chambersburg PA
CBHW060053050426
42448CB00011B/2438